# Stop Saying Yes—Negotiate!

## A Quick Reference to Better

## Your Negotiations

## Richard Devin

www13thirtybooks.com

**Stop Saying Yes – Negotiate**

**A Quick Reference to Improve Your Negotiations**

Richard Devin

Published by 13Thirty Books, Henderson Nevada, 89052 USA

www.13thirtybooks.com

ISBN:   978-0615837352

www.richarddevin.com

**13Thirty** Books

## Table of Contents

## Acknowledgement

Heather Graham, New York Times best-selling author.

Deborah Richardson, DRE&MS.

Adam Fenner.

Lance Taubold.

Eugene Menendez.

Jill Kirwen and Paul Renau.

Judith and Daniel MacGregor

 – each a mentor and friend, extraordinaire.

# ne·go·ti·ate
*v.* **ne·go·ti·at·ed, ne·go·ti·at·ing, ne·go·ti·ates**
*v.intr.*

To confer with another or others in order to come to
terms or reach an agreement

## Introduction

You *can* become a better negotiator. It makes no difference if you negotiate only at garage sales or are the family negotiator at home or a professional negotiator for a major company. You *can* become a better negotiator.

The first step in becoming a better negotiator is to understand why we, especially in the United States and other Western countries, don't like to negotiate. If I were to ask any group of people why we don't negotiate, we would all devise a list of reasons we have for not negotiating. Here are a few examples:

- It's not done that way in the United States.

- It's embarrassing.

- It's not worth it.

- It's cheap.

- You can't do that!

- That's like stealing.

7

- I didn't know I could.

- We negotiate only for automobiles and houses.

- I have the money, so why bother?

One could argue that at least some of these statements on why we do not negotiate are partly true. That does not mean, however, that some negotiation cannot take place, or at least, be attempted. Our self-doubts—our self-negotiations, more than those with whom we want to negotiate, hold us back far too often from negotiating.

Now, lest you think that we only devise these and many other excuses not to negotiate on the personal side of negotiating, let me share this with you. In the last several years, I have conducted workshops and seminars on The Art of Negotiations for countless Fortune 500 Company executives, sales departments, purchasing departments, marketing departments, Internet technology, information technology, and human resources departments. Some of these people are the presidents or vice presidents of divisions, and there have been many CEOs, CFOs, and owners of major sales organizations. One would think that these professional negotiators—many at the top of their game—would not have a single excuse why you should not or could not negotiate. Then, you would be wrong.

If you're reading this book because you want to become a better negotiator in your life, it might be heartening for you to read on. Not only negotiators dealing with the personal side of negotiating, that is, buying a house or an automobile, have an excuse why they should not or cannot negotiate. Those who negotiate for a living—professional negotiators—also devise a list of excuses. The following are just a few reasons—excuses—professional negotiators say they should not, would not, or could not negotiate:

- It's too small a deal.

- I would rather build a relationship.

- Why risk it?

- The other side said, "Yes." So let's just close the deal.

- What more can I get?

- I don't want the other side to think I'm greedy.

- I want the other side to be satisfied.

- We are aiming for a win-win situation.

- My management said they wanted me to *work* with this organization.

- It was a quick and easy negotiation. Why push it?

- They're much too good a customer to ruin with a negotiation.

- The last time we attempted to negotiate with them, they took us to the cleaners.

- Oh, we would, but they don't negotiate.

- We asked them and they said no.

- Negotiate? We just don't do that.

And it goes on.

I hear, at least, one "new one" at every workshop I present. After every workshop, I've heard the last "excuse," then, next session, there's a new one. If I told you that negotiating is easy, how would you respond? If I asked what prevents *you* from negotiating, or what prevents *us all* from negotiating, how would you answer?

You might think that you know why we don't negotiate, but I will tell you the real reason. It's one word, one small word—**no**! That's it. A small word, certainly, but if you believe it, a powerful small word. None of us wants to hear that word.

The biggest obstacle to your ability to negotiate is your fear of *no*. It affects all negotiators, from those who negotiate for a baker's dozen to those who negotiate a multimillion-dollar deal. *No* is so powerful that it not only affects your ability to ask for something, it can also take away your ability to use your power. *No* not only prevents you from using your power, but it also takes power away from you and gives it to the other side. Each time you do not ask because the answer might be *no*, you give the other side power.

Understanding *no* is the key to your understanding your ability to negotiate. *No* is not an end to a request. *No* does not mean that I won't do what you ask of me. Now, this might be politically incorrect, but *No* does not always mean no, at least about negotiations. *No* means you need to ask me differently.

Before you can ask me for something, however, you need to know what my strategy is. Who am I? What do I want from you? What pressures are there on me? You need to know from where I'm coming.

Answering these questions and understanding *no* are the keys that unlock a successful negotiation. If you know from where *I come*, you will greatly improve *your* negotiation. And if you know a bit more about me, that is, my negotiating strategy, you will greatly improve *our* negotiation.

Notice, in the last sentence, that I said *our* negotiation. That's right. Your power lies in the knowledge you have or the knowledge you can get. The more you know about the other side, the better *our* negotiations will be. Your chances of walking away with your targets met and the other side walking away more satisfied with the negotiation greatly improve by knowing from where the other side is coming.

I'm asked at every workshop, seminar, book signing, and dinner party I've ever attended, "How can making one side a better negotiator enhance the negotiation for both sides?" The answer lies in the satisfaction level you, the educated negotiator, and the other side feel after the negotiations have been completed. If you make the other side work harder, they might feel better about what they received from the negotiation. And that holds, even if what the other side receives is far less than their original targets and aspiration levels. Make them work harder, make them negotiate more, and they will feel much more satisfied about what they *gave up* during the negotiation.

In the following pages, I have broken down the strategies of many types of negotiators and negotiating tactics. You will instantly recognize some, and I'm sure one is *you*. I've given these strategies names. Names that will make it easier for you to recognize a particular negotiating style. Names, too, serve another purpose. Names not only make it easier for you to remember a strategy, one that you might wish to use in your next negotiation, but perhaps, more important, names also allow you to recognize and defend yourself from a negotiating strategy the other side attempts to use on you. As with the great battles of war, if you don't know what you're up against, you cannot defend yourself.

## Think Before You Speak

There's a significant problem with all negotiations—*you have to say something!* The simple act of speaking, of conveying an idea, is a major power transfer in any negotiation. Whenever you open your mouth and speak, you give power away. The power transfer is not in *what you intended to say*, but rather in *what you did not mean to say*. And you, the negotiator, are not the only one giving away your power. The others you work with give that power—your power— away. Note, I said, "working with," not working against. Anyone on your side, those on your team, might be giving away *your* power.

How? You're on the buying side, and you have just been told that a large shipment of a much-needed product will not happen. The seller could not secure the product in the quantity you had contracted. Before you can deal with the breach-of-contract problems, you must find a replacement product. Immediately, you're on the phone communicating with other suppliers. You leave messages with several, trying to sound as calm and cool as you can.

Once you've left the last voice-mail message, you hang up the telephone and head to the company receptionist. You inform the receptionist at your organization that you are waiting for a few salespeople from several companies who can get you the products, in the quantities you need, to call you back. You tell the receptionist that she is to interrupt you immediately, when any of these salespeople call. You make your way to the next meeting or back to your office to settle down to work.

Soon, a call from the company receptionist comes in, and she dutifully tells you that a salesperson from one supplier is on the line. You pick up the phone, ready to play it cool, when the first words out of the salesperson's mouth are, "So, your receptionist tells me, let me get this right, you just lost a big order, and you're scrambling to fill it."

Now, it might have been a good idea for not only you to practice the Think Before You Speak rule—perhaps you gave the receptionist more information than you should have—but also for everyone in your organization to *know* this rule. Knowing the rule is one thing; the problem is **not** using it. *Think Before You Speak* is a difficult rule to master.

Let's face it; we like to talk, and we especially like to talk when someone is willing to listen. The person willing to listen, however, might not be someone with your best interest in mind. It might be the competition or the other side with whom you're about to negotiate. You talk; they listen, and they gain power. If you *think before you speak*, and you *listen when they speak*, you and your negotiation will gain power. The first rule of negotiating is to shut up. When you shut up, the other side talks.

Here's the next step. Listen. You have to listen to gain power. What's the difficulty with the Think Before You Speak rule? Often, *I shut up*, but *I don't listen*. Instead, I think about what I want to say next! I think about my response. I think about, or plan, my argument against what you say. I don't listen to what you say. I only listen to my internal dialogue, practicing what I will say to you when you stop talking. Don't do this!

Shut up.

Listen.

Think.

Then, respond.

## Ask

In the preceding chapter, I wrote that *Think Before You Speak* is the first rule of negotiations. Because *Think Before You Speak* is the first rule, *Ask* is its twin. Why don't we get the things we want in life? In business? In negotiations? Because we don't ask!

I am amazed how many skilled negotiators I've met over the years will leave a mock negotiation conducted in my seminars, dissatisfied, because they did not get a concession they had set as one of their targets. When I ask the other negotiators in these mock negotiations why they were so unwilling to give in on that concession, more frequently than not, they tell me that the negotiator on the other team never asked for it. Does that surprise you? It surprised me.

When I've asked those in the seminars why we don't get the concession we want, I get excuses such as the following: "They were not receptive." "I tried, but they wouldn't listen." "They had all the power."

My next question to the group is, "Did you ask?" And the

responses this time include:

- "Well, sort of."

- "I couldn't."

- "I didn't think I should take the chance."

- "We could have done that, if only we had more time."

- "I didn't know much about the other side."

- "I didn't know we could."

All these statements, questions, could have been settled easily if the negotiators had done one thing—**ask**.

Why don't we ask? As I said earlier, we don't ask nearly enough because of one little word that packs much power—*no!* We dread hearing it, so we isolate ourselves from it. If we don't ask, they can't say no.

Before, during, and after every negotiation, you should

- Ask—those on your team

- Ask—the other side

- Ask—yourself

By asking those on your team or those on the other side's team or even asking yourself, three things can happen, and in each case, bringing more power to you.

Ask, and you get a—yes! Great. Now, ask for more. That's right. Don't stop there; you have them in the *Yes Zone*. Try for something else. In the following chapters, you'll discover how even asking for something you do not want could be beneficial to the overall negotiation.

Ask, and you get a—maybe. Great, again. Now, work them. Discover if the *maybe* is a tactic or if the other side just needs to be convinced a bit more. Perhaps they need more time. Continue to ask. Is there something preventing them from saying yes now? Whatever the answer to this question is—brings power to you.

Ask and get—no! Not so great, but not bad, either. You've discovered something. Perhaps you're not asking the right way. You see, *no* is not the end to your request. It might mean that you have to ask differently.

- Does the no mean—that your request is out of order?
- Does the no mean—that your request is a concession the other side is *unwilling* to give?

- Does the no mean—a request the other side *cannot* give?

By hearing *no*, you have been given the opportunity to explore the possibilities. You ask. You get a response. Now, you ask again. Every time the other side responds to your requests, you gain information. Information is power.

Ask. Then, shut up and listen. You're about to be told the possibilities—possibilities and information that later might lead to more power or to other concessions. And those are concessions that you might never have had the opportunity to receive, or to explore, if you had not taken a moment to ask. Now, let's take this one step further and not only ask for something, but also ask for something you have no desire to obtain.

## Asking for Something You Don't Want

I have found, through the many mock negotiations I have conducted in my seminars and workshops, that this tactic, the strategy of *Asking for Something You Don't Want*, is a difficult tactic for most negotiators to put to work. So, why, if this tactic is so difficult to put to work, and the negotiation you're in is already proceeding nicely, would I want you to *Ask for Something You Don't Want?*

Why would anyone want to jeopardize a negotiation proceeding well by asking for a concession from the other side—that is not wanted? Think about that. Why would you ask the other side for something you do not want, need, or desire? What you're asking the other side for might be worthless to you. It might even be a concession that, if granted, could cause some burden to you or your organization.

You might spend much time on this request. You might even make an issue of asking for this concession by playing on the Presentation Value (I'll discuss this in an upcoming chapter). All for something you do not want. Because if you do, you stand a great chance of gaining information. And remember, *information is power*. You can learn so much by asking for something you don't want.

What if you had started this negotiation by asking for a concession you do not want, and the other side readily gave it to you? You have just gained power. Now, you just got a concession you don't want from the other side. And you're thinking, great! Getting a concession you do not want from the other side is ... power? Yes.

How is this concession power? Its power is in the fact you have just discovered that this concession might mean little to the other side, which could be why they gave it to you. Or perhaps, the other side gave you this concession because they hoped that it would set up an amicable negotiation, one in which you would see that they are willing to work with you. And they might hope that the concession they just gave in to will result in obligation on your part and, thus, cause you to give a concession to them.

Those are all great expectations. Good logic is in this approach, which is a fine way to proceed with a negotiation. The problem with these hopes is that you might not have taken these concessions the other side made to you in the same way they thought you would.

You might be thinking?

- The concession the other side just gave to you means little to them.

- The other side gave in too easily—now, what else can you get?

- The other side didn't want to spend time on this concession, and perhaps, they have something bigger in mind. Now, your defenses are up.

- You might now think that the other side *has* to work with you, and they must close this deal, so they gave a little to show their willingness to deal.

- You might also see that the other side gave in too easily, and now, you believe that they are not skilled negotiators, so you change your strategy and now will walk all over them.

- In addition, you've also learned a bit about the other side's time constraints. If they are willing to spend time on this concession, they might have more time available than you had thought.

- And you might now begin to recognize, especially if this is the first time you and the other side have met at the negotiating table or if this negotiation has been in progress for only a short period, how the other side works.

From these bits of information—*power*—you can better plan to work against the other side. Once you get a feel for the tone and style of the other side's negotiations, they might even reveal to you some of their negotiating tactics and strategies.

Now, remember that you have achieved all this by asking for a concession meaning little or nothing to you. If you ask and don't get the concession, what have you lost? Time, perhaps, but in the end, you've gained so much information that you cannot help having a better overall negotiation. More power to you. Now, you've gained much information, and you got a concession you have no desire to keep, or one for which you have no need. So what do you do with this concession?

Give it back! You read that correctly. You get a concession that means little or nothing to you from the other side, and now, you're going to give it back? What is the other side going to think? What is your organization's management going to think? You can already hear what your boss will say to you when you get back to the office. Your team reports to your management that you spent so much time and energy at the negotiation's beginning on receiving a concession that you didn't want or need, then to add insult to injury—you gave it back.

Once, this concession was worthless. Worthless, that is, unless you make it mean something to the other side, for example: Let us say that you and I have been negotiating my employment contract, and I have just asked that several additional days be added to my paid vacation. You are the human resources director of the company, and you have the authority to give me additional days in vacation time. You agree that I am a great employee, and it would not cause a hardship to the organization to give me the additional days in vacation time.

"Great," I say. Not because I'm happy to get the additional paid days included in my vacation, but because I now know that you have the authority to make a concession to me, and that the organization can make these days available with pay.

What you don't know, and remember you're the human resources director here, is that I don't want more time off. I just wanted to see if you value me enough, as an employee, to give me more time off. And guess what I've found out? You do. Now, I've gained power.

So I tell you, "I don't want the additional paid vacation days. It was a great gesture on your part to give them to me, and I appreciate the added time off, but because I rarely take long vacations, I would like to give you back those paid days off for a higher pay rate." What would you, the human resources director, say to that?

Think about it. As an employee, I have just gained everything by asking for something I did not want. I might walk away from this negotiation having gained several additional paid vacation days. And as the human resources director, you have benefited, because we both leave the negotiation feeling satisfaction. I know that I'm a valued employee, and you might have saved the company some money by giving in on the paid days off and holding firm on the higher pay rate. In the end, asking for something you don't need might be what you needed.

## Ask, Don't Tell

You see an ad in the local newspaper for an automobile, reading:

2004 Ford Expedition. 10K miles. Automatic. Anti-lock brakes. Four-wheel drive. Dark metallic blue paint. Legal tinted windows. Full power, including Driver seat, Passenger seat, Windows, Door locks, Mirrors, Headrests. Complete leather interior. Bird's-eye maple wood trim. 3rd row seat. Like new. Asking $26,900.

The year is right. The mileage is right. The color is right. The condition is right. And, most important, the price is right. So you call the seller to set up an appointment to test-drive the vehicle.

You arrive to check out the Expedition. It's perfect. You can picture yourself driving it, cruising along the interstate. The interior is in perfect condition, not a nick or stain; it's plush, comfortable, and you want it. Now, it's time to start negotiating. You open the negotiation by saying, "The ad in the newspaper said that you were asking $26,900. How firm are you?"

Anything wrong with the negotiation so far? All you've done is quote the newspaper advertisement to the seller. What harm can come from a statement that quotes the obvious? The ad did state, "Asking $26,900."

You didn't give away any information about your position by reading back the advertisement. You didn't let on about how much you want this vehicle. You just started a conversation—a negotiation —with the seller. If you were to say that nothing is wrong with this opening, you might be right; you didn't give away any information about you. Then, you might be wrong because you gave power away.

How so? Because, you bought into the other side's rules. You allowed the other side to establish the playing field. "Just by reading back the advertisement from the newspaper?" I can hear you ask.

That's right. *The Ask, Don't Tell* rule is a simple rule once mastered, but when ignored or forgotten, we fall into this trap. We negotiate based on information the other side has supplied to us. We begin right where the other side would like us to begin.

Let's try again, using the Ford Expedition advertisement, and see what happens when we negotiate from information supplied by the other side. You want this Expedition, and after checking it thoroughly,

you really want it. Based on the advertisement in the newspaper,

you start the negotiation by asking the seller if the $26,900 price tag is

firm.

OK, now that you've done that, the vehicle's seller can have

several responses. He could respond with

- That price is a great price for this car. So yes, it is firm."

- "What were you thinking of offering?"

- "There might be some room to give a little … make

me an offer."

Each statement above keeps the seller in control. He keeps the

power by asking you to make the first concession. All this happens

because, as the prospective buyer, *you* told the seller how much *he* is

asking for the vehicle, instead of asking him what he's intending to get

for the vehicle.

What would have happened if you took the same set of

circumstances, but instead of telling the seller what *you know*, you asked

him what *he knows?* Start the negotiation by saying, "I like the car, and

if the price is right, I'd take it. What were you asking for it?"

How does that opening differ from the earlier opening statement? Let's compare the two.

Opening statement #1. "The advertisement in the newspaper said that you were asking $26,900. How firm are you?"

Opening statement #2. "I like the car, and if the price were right, I'd take it. What are you asking for it?"

In statement #1, you *told* the seller how much he was asking for the vehicle, then asked if there was any room to negotiate. In statement #2, you *asked* the seller of the Expedition what the asking price was. It might not seem like much of a distinction, but let's look at what happens to the beginning of the negotiation in both cases.

In the first case, the seller will negotiate from what price? $26,900. Right? Why is that? Because you told him to. *The advertisement in the newspaper said that you were asking $26,900. How firm are you?*

In the second case, the seller has to tell you what he wants for the vehicle. *I like the car, and if the price were right, I'd take it. What were you asking for it?*

In truth, it might not be anything less than the seller had listed in the advertisement. The seller might come back to you with, "I'm asking $26,900." On the other hand, the seller might come back to you with something that might be substantially less than was listed in the advertisement. The seller might say something to the effect of, "I'm asking $26,900, but I'm willing to negotiate." Or, "I'm asking $26, 900, but if you take it today, I'll let it go for $26,000." You've just received a concession from the seller, and you haven't even begun to negotiate. If that happens, you must now ask yourself, "How much more room does the seller have to negotiate on price?" and "What pressures are there on the seller that you are unaware of?"

You don't know what is happening in the seller's world. There might be huge pressures on him to sell that Expedition today... now. And by starting the negotiation with statement #1, *The advertisement in the newspaper said that you were asking $26.900. How firm are you?* you will never learn what pressures there might be. The seller has no reason to tell you anything because you just told him what the starting price is on this Expedition, and then you gave him more power by saying, "How firm are you?"

If the seller were to respond with, "I'm very firm on the price," where can you go? And at what price would you then begin the negotiation? His price. In statement #2, *I like the car, and if the price were right, I'd take it. What are you asking for it?* you're leaving the question of price open. By doing so, you ask the seller for the first concession, and you give the seller an opportunity to make the first concession. Whatever his response might be, you have gained information.

    *Ask, Don't Tell*, and the seller's response might surprise you.

## Aspiration Levels

We all have aspirations. The Merriam-Webster Dictionary describes aspirations this way: "A strong desire to achieve something high or great; An object of desire." During every negotiation, aspiration levels constantly change. Everything you say and do in a negotiation drives the other side's aspiration levels in a particular direction.

Because everything *you* say and do affects the other side's aspiration levels, it must be true that everything the other side says and does affects your aspiration levels. And the frightening thing is that not only the other side affects *your* aspiration levels. Everything you say and do in a negotiation to affect the other side also affects your aspiration levels. Both your side and the other side continually drive aspiration levels up or down—*for both sides.*

In any negotiation, you want the other side to lower their aspiration levels. It should be a key to your negotiating strategy. What you forget, however, is that what *you* say and do can have the effect of negotiating *on yourself* for the other side. In effect, you negotiate against yourself, which happens because you affect *your* aspiration levels and targets by what *you* say to the other side.

Think about that. Have you ever said something about a product or service that made you start to think that the price the seller asked was not such a bad price after all? If so, you have negotiated for the other side against yourself. You have begun to think or act in a way that affects your aspiration levels. And in doing so, you have lowered your aspirations and agreed with the other side, convincing yourself that paying more is worth it. You talked yourself into it, which is precisely what you want to do to the other side. Allow them to *talk themselves into it.*

Aspiration levels constantly change throughout any negotiation. Your job is to recognize when your aspiration levels change, and then to consider that change before making a concession or even a statement. Remember the *Think Before You Speak* rule.

You should also be aware of how the other side's aspiration levels change, either by what *you* say and do or by what *they* say and do, which is much like a game of poker. You watch for the other side's "tells." Is the other side beginning to negotiate with themselves on your behalf?

If so, their aspiration levels have changed, which is the perfect time to *Ask for Something You Don't Want.*

As discussed in an earlier chapter, *Think Before You Speak,* the other side might be telling you something. Aspiration levels might be expressed as *expectations.* What are *you* expecting? What are *they* expecting? Common enough questions, but in a negotiation, you should ask yourself these questions whenever you're about to speak, and then, just after you've spoken. Do not make a statement until you have discovered what your expectations are, both from the other side's response, and then from your response.

Be prepared for the possible responses. In doing so, you can control your *Aspiration Levels.* Controlling your *Aspiration Levels* also will control or affect the other side's *Aspiration Levels,* all to your benefit.

## Presentation Value

As discussed in the previous chapter, one of our goals in any negotiation is to find a means to affect the other side's *Aspiration Levels.* The *Presentation Value* you bring to a negotiation will have that much-desired effect. I spent many years as an actor, and those years have served me well in all my negotiations. Like the poker game that I alluded to in a previous chapter, we have "tells." Tells are signs that might give away our intentions, our moods, and possibly our next move in a poker game or, likewise, in a negotiation.

While an actor trains and hones his acting skills, he learns to control and manipulate those tells. Every good actor learns to show what he wants to show and to hide what he does not want you to see. You need to learn to do just that in all your negotiations. *You need to become an actor.*

I would even go so far as recommending that every person in your organization involved in any form of negotiations take an acting class or two. The reason? Everything said and done in any negotiation directly affects your aspiration levels. And as discussed in the previous chapter, if it affects your aspiration levels, then it affects the other side's aspiration levels. That's right. The *Presentation Value* you bring to the negotiation affects the other side's ability to negotiate.

Watch any good actor in a film, television show, or stage production, and you will see the art of negotiating take place. *For every action, there must be an equal and opposite reaction.* Every good actor always plans what the other actor's reaction will be—just as you must in a negotiation.

Think of yourself as an actor in a play during your next negotiation. Your job is to react to what the other side says. Now, think about that reaction. Think about it before you react! How will it affect the other side's aspiration levels? Is it driving those aspiration levels up, and thus the hopes of the other side, or is it driving aspiration levels down? To affect the other side's aspiration levels, you must act and react as though some outside force were directing you.

In films, television and on the stage, that outside force would be the director and the other actors. In a negotiation, that outside force is the drive to close the deal. And not simply to close the deal—anyone can do that—but to close the deal where you can bring about the best possible outcome for you and your organization. That outside force must also drive the other side's aspiration levels so they leave the negotiation feeling that they have achieved their aspiration levels.

Shakespeare wrote, "All the world is a stage." You must be an actor on that stage in every negotiation. Preparing for your acting debut prepares for the negotiation. What does an actor do before the play opens or the audience is allowed in? He rehearses, and you must. Just as an actor, you must learn your lines, practice your responses, note your body language, and "block" the scene. No one should ever enter into a negotiation without first rehearsing the scene.

Think about this—if I invited you to go to a Broadway show, to a movie, or even to a screening of the newest hit sitcom, you might well say yes. Then, I tell you that the tickets to this Broadway show, movie, or the special screening of the new sitcom are very expensive. Then, I say to you that the actors in this production have never seen the script, and they have never rehearsed, and they have had no director. Would you still want to pay a hefty price for the ticket? Most of us would say no. Why would any of us want to pay a large sum of money to see an unrehearsed, unscripted play, television series, or movie?

The same must hold for you in a negotiation. Why would you, or should you, expect your organization to pay a hefty price for you to enter into a negotiation for which you are unprepared? Every negotiation should have a rehearsal.

For some negotiations, it can be as simple as pairing with someone to play the other side, then acting out the negotiation. For other negotiations, you should put together a cast, a team complete with a director who can listen to the mock negotiation and then advise the team. Have members of your organization play both sides. Switch those cast members around, so every person is on your team's side, then on the other team's side. I guarantee that you and your organization will find that it is time well spent and money well saved.

In these mock negotiations, you will find answers to questions you might not have been prepared to answer, and you will find questions you might not have been prepared to ask—questions the other side might not be prepared to answer. Why? Because they didn't rehearse.

These mock negotiations will also shed light on weaker areas of your negotiations: your vulnerabilities, your team's vulnerabilities, your organizations vulnerabilities—those chinks in the armor that might allow the other side to gain or even take control of the negotiation—and thus, give them power. Rehearse, and your next negotiation will be a guaranteed award winner.

## Reasonable and Ridiculous

I have several questions I would like you to ponder before you read on, and you should be prepared to answer these questions before your next negotiation.

1. What is reasonable?

2. What is ridiculous?

3. Who determines what is reasonable or ridiculous?

Surprisingly, during most negotiations, *you* are the person, or the negotiator, who determines what is reasonable and what is ridiculous. That doesn't sound too bad, until you realize that you are not determining reasonable and ridiculous to limit the other side's negotiating power—you're making that decision to limit yourself! How did you do that? Through self-negotiation.

Typically, in a negotiation's planning stages, we try to determine some guidelines to help us navigate the negotiation highway. as we know, this might not be an easy path, which is why we plan and rehearse. However, those plans, that often help us a great deal in navigating through a negotiation can also take power away from us. Instead of guiding us in the right direction, they can lead us astray. How? By placing limits on our power to negotiate fully with the other side.

In determining reasonable and ridiculous, you have decided for the other side without allowing the other side in on the decision making. Now, in truth, this is not always a bad move; it can be very beneficial to your negotiation if done properly and without prejudice to your side. Often, however, *your* determination of what is reasonable and ridiculous limits *you,* not *the other side.*

For example, I'm selling a product. You need this product. Vendors are competing in the marketplace, so you have at least one other vendor from whom to buy. Through your research, you and your organization have determined that the other vendor's products do not match my product in terms of price and quality. Therefore, my product is the one you prefer.

The negotiations begin, and you make an offer to me. With pricing, where is that offer? Is it just under my quote? Well below my quote? Over my quote?

## Stop Saying Yes – Negotiate!

Of course, real-world elements here might play into where you begin, but despite where you are—under, over, or right at my quote—in your opening offer, how much room did you leave yourself to negotiate? This is precisely where the two R's of reasonable and ridiculous trap you. How much room is there in your opening offer to negotiate? Perhaps I should ask, did you leave any room to negotiate?

Let's say that the product I'm selling has been quoted to you at $1,000 a piece. You know that there is room for me to negotiate with you on price. How do you know this? Because you and your team have done the research and planning for this negotiation and know that similar products sell between $875 and $1,150, slightly over and under my asking price of $1,000 a piece. Given this information, where would you make your first offer? That is, what would you determine to be a reasonable opening offer? Would anything between $875 and $1,000 be a reasonable opening offer?

OK, let's say that you came in at $925. You have changed the course of the negotiations in two ways, right off the bat, by making an opening offer of $925.

1.  You left yourself some room to negotiate.

2.   But you also gave the selling side a concession.

That's right. You made a concession to the selling side, and they did not even have to ask for it. And to make matters worse, you might not even know that you did it.

What is that concession? During your market research, you've determined that this product I'm selling or similar products are priced between $875 and $1,150. If so, why isn't your opening offer at $875? Why isn't your opening offer even lower than $875? Because you decided on an opening offer to me that *you* felt was reasonable. And the other side thanks you for that. You just made a concession. Now, you're doing the work for the other side!

When you determined what would be a reasonable price to pay for this product, you were working for the other side, negotiating with yourself to the benefit of the other side. *You were making decisions that place limitations on your power.* Those limitations prevent you from negotiating to the fullest, not because the other side took power, but because you gave the other side the power.

What I'm suggesting to you is that you do not act reasonably. Whenever you think you're being reasonable, take a step back, think about what being reasonable will do to this and future negotiations. Be prepared to make an offer you think is unreasonable or even ridiculous. Weigh the alternatives.

- What's going to happen to this negotiation if I come in with a ridiculous opening offer?
- How will it affect the other side's targets and aspirations levels?
- What might this opening offer do to your future negotiations with this organization or with this negotiator?

You indeed might find that a ridiculous offer will kill the negotiation—that the other side might just dismiss the issue, and perhaps even you. But there is so much to gain—so much information (power) to be gained from making what the other side might see as a ridiculous opening or counteroffer.

What if you made a ridiculous opening offer and the other side

- Walked away?
- Didn't walk, but countered?

What do you know about them that you didn't know before?

If they walked, you now know that they have the power to buy or sell, and they don't need to buy or sell from you. If they didn't walk, but countered, you now know that they might have time constraints. They might need this sale. They might want to work with you. There might be problems with the company. All this information is now yours because you were willing and able to make a ridiculous opening offer.

Leave yourself open to the idea of going into the negotiation being ridiculous. Don't become trapped, and thus limit your power by your ideas of what is reasonable and what is ridiculous. Make the other side work for every concession. Don't do the work *for* them.

## Don't Turn a Buyer into a Shopper

I was ready to purchase an iron gate for the entrance to my courtyard. There is direct access from the front of the house and street to the inner courtyard, and I felt a simple, but nicely designed, gate would not only enhance the look of the entrance, but would also add a sense of security. I did not want anything too fancy, just a gate that split in the middle and opened both into the courtyard and out toward the street.

I drove around my neighborhood to get a few ideas, searching out other houses that had courtyards and gates. I also checked out a few ironwork companies in the area for pricing and design ideas. From my conversations with my neighbors and the salespeople at the ironworks companies, I thought a gate, designed as I have said, should cost me about $500. I had budgeted $750, so I did have some room to negotiate. I had set up an appointment with a representative from a local iron works company to come by the house to take measurements and to give me an estimate.

Pat was a nice enough person and we had a pleasant conversation before I told him what I wanted for the entrance to the courtyard. I not only told him what I was looking for, but I had also drawn a crude, but effective, representation of the gate I wanted to have built and installed. Pat did a few calculations and said that it would be no problem—"An easy job. We'll have it built and installed in less than three days." Then, he hit me with, "And it will cost you $436."

I was very pleased. The $436 Pat just quoted fell well in the $500 I thought it would cost, and the $750 I had budgeted for it. I was at first tempted to jump in and take Pat's bid. But being the good negotiator that we should be, I didn't say yes; I negotiated.

After giving Pat's quote a few minutes of thought, I decided to see if there was any room to negotiate with Pat's bid. "Boy," I said, "that's more than I was thinking of spending on this. Pat, your design is good, and I feel comfortable buying from you, but my neighbor down the street had a gate put in for about 100 bucks less." Now, although that was true, the gate was much smaller, designed to keep his dogs in the backyard. But if Pat didn't ask me about the specifics of my neighbor's gate, was it up to me to tell him?

"Oh?" Pat responded. "Let's see then." Pat rechecked his numbers. "Yeah, I think we can do a little better with that price. How's $354 sound?"

How did it sound? I was ecstatic. That was a great price. My first thought was, where do I sign? Then, it hit me. Pat came in at $436. Then, with only one request from me to lower the price, he dropped to $354. What will he do if I ask again—give *me* a check?

I started to question how much profit Pat was trying to make off me. How much should this gate cost? Suddenly, I was no longer concerned with buying a gate today. My only thought now was how much I should be spending.

Instead of securing a buyer, Pat had driven one away by turning me from a buyer into a shopper. No way would I order that gate today. Instead of buying, I was going shopping.

When Pat asked for my signature on the purchase order, he was shocked when I said, "Not yet, I need to look around a bit more." The look on his face said it all. He knew that he had given in too much, too quickly, and had done it all without making me work for the concessions. He had indeed turned a buyer into a shopper.

Make the other side work for every concession you are prepared to give them. Far too often, we want to close the deal quickly. Pressures on us might not be evident to the other side. If you give too much, too soon, you are letting the other side gain information—power—the other side did not have until you gave it to them.

The first step in your concession making is to make all your concessions minor concessions. Next, you must make the other side work for every concession—however small. If you don't, you risk turning your buyer into a shopper, and in the end, a buyer for someone else.

Did I buy a gate? You bet I did, and I paid more than the $436 Pat originally asked. Why? Because, though I had become a shopper, a new concern arose—time. Time had now become more important to me than the gate's cost. I might have paid more for the gate than the $436 Pat charged, but I still paid less than I had budgeted. In the end, I was satisfied with the negotiations and with buying.

Why didn't I call Pat back and buy the gate from him at less than the other iron works company wanted? Simple, I would never buy from Pat because I didn't trust him. In turning a buyer into a shopper, he also turned me from a trusting consumer into a doubtful one. I cannot help thinking that either Pat was trying to rip me off with some huge profit built into the gate, or perhaps something was wrong with the work he said his company could do. I wasn't willing to take the risk. Because of Pat's quick concession to me, a concession I did not have to work for, another salesperson for another company made a good sale.

## Time

What can we say about time, other than *we never have enough of it?* In most negotiations, time is crucial. That is especially true in Western culture. We all know the adage, *time is money.*

What does that mean? *Time is money.* Regarding negotiations, how is time money? Think about that, and when you've answered, read on.

Now that you've thought about it, I would bet that one example you've thought of is time is money because the more time we spend on a negotiation, product, or sale, the more it's costing us. Concluding a negotiation when we have a price good for us and for the other side is much better for our side. We might lose money on a deal that takes us too long to conclude. If you answered this way, you would be right, but you would also be wrong!

For many organizations in Western culture, the result must justify the time spent.

The less time I spend in this negotiation, the better the results will be for my side. Less money will be spent negotiating, and we get the deal closed quickly and move on.

In many other cultures, outside the West, the negotiating strategy is *the more time I spend with you the more you will want to close this deal.* The more you want to close, the more money you will be willing to spend. Time, then, is money... more money for my side because you want to close. Think about how using time as a negotiating tool *against the other side*, instead of *against ourselves*, can change the negotiation's scope.

Most of us want to get in, negotiate, and get out. That's power, but not power for your side. It's power for the other side. Power you give away.

Time is your enemy in this type of negotiation. Your self-imposed time limitations work against you. You want to get in and get out quickly. If the other side notices these time constraints—which they will—you will get what you wanted, a quick deal but one you pay for dearly.

If the other side wants to get in and out of the negotiation quickly, time is your friend. Time is power. But consider this—just because you *can* close the deal now does not mean that you *should* close the deal now. True, the other side wants to get in and get out, concluding the deal as quickly as possible. You have time on your side.

So now, you should use time as a tool to gain concessions in your negotiations. Ask for concessions from the other side. Make them work for the quick deal they want. In effect, make the other side spend time to close this deal quickly, time they do not have. You will play on their self-imposed time pressures, and your negotiations will be better for it.

Do not close quickly just to make the other side happy. I can guarantee that will not happen. Oh sure, the other side might leave the negotiating table happy—because you made a quick deal with them— but just wait until they get back to their office and report to management. Their management will question the negotiation's elements. Yes, they will be pleased with a quick close, but a quick close will not seem a smart deal after management examines the deal's other elements.

The other side—that left the negotiation satisfied—will grow more dissatisfied with the deal over time. They will second-guess the negotiation's elements, and the next time you and they meet, they will be resentful. Time is not only a negotiating component during the negotiation, but also remains a component long after.

Most negotiators in sales departments would tell you that *when you get a yes, close the deal and get out of there.* The sales side has told me countless times that *to stay in a negotiation past the time the other side says yes is pure folly.* Their thoughts are, in the end, staying with the negotiation after you have a yes will have only taken more time, cost more, and possibly killed the deal. There is truth in this thinking.

Spending more time in a negotiation after the yes is indeed riskier. But a little more time spent in the negotiation will possibly bring about a better deal for you and a better feeling of satisfaction for both sides at the close of the deal. Consider the other side's time concerns, not just yours. There is power in time, but you have to use it. Make time a key in the negotiation, and give power to your side.

## The Three Tenses of Any Negotiation

Negotiations are not just about now! Every negotiation has a past, a present, and a future. How you approach a particular negotiation should consider the past, the present, and the future of this negotiation and of the negotiators.

Let's discuss the past first. This negotiation is the first time you will negotiate with this organization or person. This might be a negotiation for a onetime deal. If this deal is a onetime deal, and *if you've never seen or spoken to this person before*, you might ask, *how, then, is there a past to this negotiation?* That would be a fair and honest question. But you must realize that because *you* have never negotiated with this person or this organization before does not mean that this coming negotiation has no history.

We know that, in negotiations, where there is or has been a long-term relationship, there is a history—a history between you, the negotiator, and the negotiations. What about the first-time negotiation? How can a first-time negotiation have a history or a past? At first glance, it does not. What we must do is take a second look.

Let us take a personal negotiation, for example. You see a sign for a lawn sale just around the corner from your home. You decide to check it out. When you do, you find a bicycle sitting off to one side of the yard. It's a great bike: 18-speed mountain bike, shock absorbers on the front suspension, a padded seat, 27 inches, and a lightweight aluminum frame—what you've been thinking about buying.

Did you notice anything? We've already begun to find this negotiation's past. *You've been thinking about it.* That statement alone implies that you have been doing your own negotiations for this bike.

With whom have you been negotiating? Why, yourself, of course. You have already determined, or have been giving some thought to, what price you'd like to pay, what color you want, and then the colors you can live with, if you cannot find a bike in the exact color you want.

You've been thinking—negotiating—on what size bike. How many speeds should it have? A mountain or speed bike? Look at all the negotiating that has been going on, and you didn't even know that your neighbor would have a lawn sale and put a bike up for sale.

So, a key question here is, if you've already negotiated with yourself to buy a bike, what about the person selling the bike? What has he been negotiating? And with whom? Before you've even had the chance to ask your neighbor how much he wants for this bike, many negotiations surrounding this bike have occurred.

The bike's seller has a past to his negotiations. You have a past to your negotiations, and neither of you knew that you would negotiate with each other. The past negotiations have all been internal, *self-negotiations*.

Now that we understand a bit about the *past* negotiations, you can proceed with the *present* negotiation, right? No. Now that you have the past to this negotiation figured out, we must not turn to the present, but to the *future*.

Let's take the same bike you discovered for sale at your neighbor's lawn sale. You have decided that you would like to buy a bike, and through your dissection of your past negotiations with yourself, you have determined that you indeed would like to purchase this bike.

Now, put yourself in the position of the current bike owner, with whom you will be negotiating. What might he be thinking about this bike? Price? That he never used it? That he cannot wait to get this bike out of his garage? You should also consider what your neighbor is considering about the future. What might the future of this negotiation be, if he sells this bike to you? How will these and other questions about you and your neighbor's thoughts affect the coming negotiation with you for this bike?

For example, put yourself in the future, and let us say that you have purchased this bike from your neighbor. What would happen if this bike turned out *not* to be all you thought? What if the shocks on the front suspension bar, that you thought looked so cool, turned out to make you sick? The constant up-and-down motion at the front of the bike made you queasy, almost seasick. You've reached the point where you can't even think about getting on this bike without popping another Dramamine. Now, do you want this bike? The future isn't looking so bright.

If this were the case and the bike made you sick, could you take the bike back to your neighbor and politely explain that you would like your money back because the bike makes you throw up? How would your neighbor react to your request? What would this do to your friendship with this neighbor and perhaps your reputation throughout the neighborhood?

Now, if you had bought this bike at the local bike shop, how would they react to your situation? What would the past, present, and future of that negotiation look like? Think of all negotiations and plan all negotiations with an understanding of the *Three Tenses of Negotiations*:

• The past—How will your self-negotiations affect your current position in this negotiation?

• The future—How will this negotiation affect your future negotiations?

• The present—Knowing what you do about the past and the future, how should you proceed with this present negotiation?

Answer those questions regarding the *Three Tenses of a Negotiation*, and you will be better prepared and have more power when you enter into the actual negotiation.

## Don't Wait for the Negotiation to Begin to Begin the Negotiation

It drives me crazy. I mean it. It really drives me crazy, when I speak to a group of professional negotiators, and I learn that they are about to begin a negotiation and they have not yet begun the negotiation. What are they waiting for? Why wait at all? Why is it that negotiators wait for the negotiation to begin before they begin the negotiation? If you have the answer, e-mail me, because I haven't a clue.

In the real world, it's constantly done, that is, beginning a negotiation well before the actual, face-to-face negotiation begins. Examples abound. Look around and you will see it everywhere: in the political world, at the diplomatic embassies of this or any other nation, in the newspaper, on the web, and on television. Look, too, toward the major corporations in the United States and elsewhere—although the U.S. corporations have this tactic easily over those on foreign shores. Sometimes, we call it *advertising*, but usually, we call it *news*.

That's right. What I suggest here is that you treat your coming negotiation much as the politicians do. Make it an event. Publish it. Advertise it. Now, don't get me wrong, I don't suggest that you run out to Madison Avenue and hire an advertising agency to run a campaign for you. What I suggest is that you and your organization do it yourselves.

Let me give an example. I recently had a lunch meeting with several top executives for a nonprofit health organization to discuss a continuing negotiation. They were in the middle of a slightly messy negotiation. This organization's market share was one big plus it had going for it. It was in the high 60th percentile of the market—a very good position to be in.

The executives explained to me what was happening in the current negotiations and then asked for some feedback. They were in a delicate position of trying to limit cost increases to their clients and yet not tell the doctors what they can or cannot charge. The doctors threatened to pull out of the deal, leaving this organization's clients without medical care—at least locally—and not in the preferred hospitals and clinics.

## Stop Saying Yes – Negotiate!

The first thing I suggested to the nonprofit health care provider was to have its board of directors' draft a letter or a press release stating their strong and unwavering support for their negotiators. I told them to send that letter to everyone in the business community. In effect, advertise the board's support to the negotiators.

Why would I suggest this, and what possible benefit could they get from it? For one, a letter or press release from the board of directors to the business community would show commitment. It would also show the other side—in this case, the doctors—that the board would stand behind the negotiators' decisions, in effect, giving the negotiators of the health care organizations great power. It would also bring the business community on board and, thus, more power to the health-care negotiators.

A local news hour noticed the letter in a story they were doing on health care's rising costs. The public then became aware of the coming and continuing negotiation and made their support of the well-respected board of directors, the nonprofit health-care provider, and the business community well known. In continuing news coverage, the public and the board of directors alike expressed their sincere desire to end this negotiation in a fair agreement. The doctors' negotiators were left with little choice and felt compelled to agree with the health care provider quickly to minimize damage to the doctors' reputations and to comply with what the public and business sectors expected.

How can you advertise or publish your negotiation in a negotiation that might be on a smaller scale? This does not mean that you need to send a press release or a story to the national or local news stations as the health care provider did. Great results by advertising internally, in your organization and in the other side's organization.

Let us say that you are in a negotiation's planning stages. You and the other side have set a preliminary time to meet, the first of many meetings to come. This is the ideal time to negotiate before the negotiations begin.

How? A quick note or e-mail sent to the other side to confirm the time and place of the coming meeting and outlining the negotiation stages would indeed be negotiating before the negotiation begins. To be more elaborate, one could use Desktop Publishing to outline completely who will be attending, what will be discussed, in what order, and perhaps, who will lead the negotiation for your side. It could include press clippings of your products' benefits or of your organization's latest breakout service or awards. In short, what you do is tell the other side, before the negotiation begins, how good you are as an organization and as a negotiator. You have advertised that this negotiation will happen the way you have determined.

Be cautious not to give power away by being too bold in your advertising. Instead, slant the e-mail, letter of intent, or confirmation so the other side clearly understands your position. With a little creativity, caution, and style, you'll find that advertising your coming negotiation will give you power.

## The Glacial Response

I have a question for you. How fast does a glacier move? The answer is slowly, very slowly.

What does the speed of a glacier's movement have to do with the art of negotiating? It has *everything* to do with the *art of negotiating*. A glacier moves at the same speed you should—how quickly, or perhaps I should say how slowly, you should—move in any negotiation. Especially, when the other side makes a request of you. Any request the other side makes should be followed by the *Glacial Response*. Move slowly.

You and I are in the middle of a negotiation, and I ask you for a concession. You say to me that you would like to consider it. Now, I'm thinking that this is great. I've asked you for a concession, and you didn't say no. You said that you'd like to consider it.

What do I do next? I give you time to consider it. So you do. Then, you consider it a little more … consider it... and consider it further.

## Stop Saying Yes – Negotiate!

What does a considered response do for me, the other party, in the negotiation? I'm left with no other choice than to believe that you are thinking about the request I've just made of you. You are considering the concession I'm asking you to make. And that, to me, is a positive response to my request.

I don't want to push you on the decision, because you might be leaning my way in making the concession. If that is the case, I don't want to rock the boat. Even if you are not leaning my way in making the concession, you might be considering another concession to make to me instead. Again, I don't want to rush this decision-making process along too quickly. So I leave you to your thoughts.

You, however, are playing on my time constraints by moving like a glacier, which is power. Even if you know the answer to my request—whether a positive or a negative response—you still should move slowly. Take advantage of the power I have given you when I asked you for a concession. Move like a glacier.

In your life, how do you respond when your boss, wife, or partner says they are "thinking about it?" Sure, you can push them a little, but you don't want to upset them. You want to give them time to think. So you wait until they've "thought about it," putting you in limbo.

You've asked for a concession. They are thinking about it. So now, you wait or move on to another subject of the negotiation. The Glacial Response is a great time tactic. Whenever you hear "Let me take that under advisement," "I'm thinking about it," or "Let me take this to my director," it affects your aspiration levels. Your glacial consideration of my request for a concession might push me into conceding to you, just to move you along.

If you use the Glacial Response, the other side will think long and hard before they ask you to consider any other request. By asking you for a concession, the other side unwittingly has put you in the position of power. Take your time. Take the other side's time. And while you're thinking about the other side's request—you might wish to make a small request of your own. This is the perfect time—as discussed in an earlier chapter—to ask for something you do not want.

## Make 'Em Work

"Time is Money"—an American Corporate mantra. As discussed earlier, in almost all negotiations, we never have enough time. And if we agree *time is money*, we agree that the more time we spend on a negotiation, the more money we spend on that negotiation. Time equals money. Time spent. Money spent. Time saved. Money saved. We understand that for ourselves.

What we fail to consider in most of our negotiations is that, if time is money to us, what is time to the other side? What is true for our side must also be true for the other side. Time is money to both sides in a negotiation.

We go into a negotiation understanding our time constraints, our powers, and our weaknesses. What we often fail to recognize is that the other side might have time constraints, powers, and weaknesses even greater than ours.

The saying goes, "The more time you make the other side spend in a negotiation, the more the other side will want to close the deal." That's right. In most negotiations, time spent is money in your pocket. What we do in negotiations is focused on our side—what we need to do to close this deal. And time is often a key to our negotiations. What we should do is focus less on our time constraints and make the other side work—make them spend time and, consequently, money, on this negotiation. The more the other side invests in the negotiation, the more they will want to close this deal. Play on their time constraints.

We have all been there—down to the wire, when we've had little or no choice but to make the purchase or the sale and close the deal. Our cost in time had become too great and closing the deal now—even if not the best deal for us—saved us additional time and money, which is where you want the other side to be. Pushing the other side to the limits of their self-imposed time constraints, oddly, produces an effect that is good for us. This is the other side of time— one of satisfaction.

If I ask you for a concession and without a second's thought you give it to me, how do I feel? Put yourself in that position. You ask your boss for a raise of $200 a year. Your boss barely looks up from the pile of papers on his desk and says, "Yeah, sure thing." What happened? Are you happy?

On one hand, you got what you wanted and exactly what you asked for—a $200 a year raise. But because your boss was so quick with his response, you're less than satisfied. You might be disappointed. You cannot help but wonder if you could have gotten a bigger raise or, perhaps, something more. Why? Because your boss didn't spend any of his time, or yours, before granting the concession.

Look what Make 'em Work has done to you. It has affected your Aspiration Levels in such a way that though you left with what you asked for, you're not satisfied with it.

Time is money, and time is satisfaction. The more time the other side spends on the negotiation, the more they will want to close the deal and the more satisfied they will be with the results of the negotiation.

If your boss had used the Glacial Response to your request for a raise, you would have been happy to get the $200. You might have been happy to get a smaller raise. Why? Because you had to work for it.

Even if you can close the deal now, don't. It might be

necessary for you to stop, don't close. Instead, Make 'em Work a little longer. Just because you can close does not mean that you must close. The other side might be more satisfied to settle for less if you don't close the deal now.

## Speedy Negotiations

In the previous chapter, we discussed how powerful a tool time could be, a tool that we can and should use to our advantage, whenever possible. We discussed how spending more time in a negotiation can mean a better negotiation—not only for you, but also in the satisfaction level that the other side will have after the negotiation, all because of the time we spent. However, time has another side.

Studies show that, in general terms, the more time a negotiator spends on a negotiation, the more that negotiator will want to close the deal. It is also true, however, that sometimes, the less time we spend in a negotiation, the better our negotiation will be.

Contradictions? You bet.

Think speed.

Get in.

Begin.

Negotiate.

Get out.

Why would one want to negotiate with speed?

- It could be I don't need this deal, or I don't want the product or service, but if I can get it at a good price, I'll take it.

- It could be I'm just negotiating to learn something about the other side and the other side's organization. I'm playing detective. And in doing so, I gain valuable knowledge—power—knowledge I will hand off to other negotiators from my organization to use against you later.

- It could be I'm not a very skilled negotiator. If I think or know that you might be very good at negotiations, I do not want to spend any more time with you than I need to. If I take my time with our negotiation, I'm afraid that you'll notice any weaknesses I might have, and then use them to your great advantage, now, or in future negotiations with me.

- Perhaps changes are occurring at my organization that I do not want you and your organization to discover. So I come in and get out as quickly as possible.

- I could believe that all negotiations begin with one side

high, one side low, and we meet in the middle. So let's just get there as fast as we can.

- It could be I want to throw you off for future negotiations. After this negotiation, your side believes that my side comes in quickly and gets out just as quickly. Maybe next time, I will not negotiate so quickly. What will that do to your negotiating strategy in the future?

These are just a few possible reasons for you and your negotiating team to consider going in and negotiating quickly.

Plan to use the Speedy Negotiation tactic in all your mock negotiations. You should consider this strategy's possible uses, not only by your side, but by the other side as well. Strategize how you will react in the negotiation if the other side uses a Speedy Negotiation tactic on you.

I have found in the workshops and seminars I've conducted that the more skilled negotiator usually does a better job with Speedy Negotiations. Skilled negotiators have a confidence about themselves, enabling them to pull off a Speedy Negotiation. If you are the more skilled negotiator, then try a Speedy Negotiation. And—again, a contradiction—if you are the less skilled negotiator, surprisingly, you might want to try a Speedy Negotiation. In both cases of the skilled and of the less skilled negotiator, gains can be made, but caution here is the rule. Plan for this tactic, and use it wisely.

## The God Factor or Extreme Procurement

OK, I'm just going to say it, and those of you on the selling side of anything, I'm sure, will quickly agree. Some on the buying side think that they are a god—note, it might be god with a little "g," but in their world, they are the only. When you step into the office of a little "g" god or get them on the phone, they make sure that you know, without a doubt, that you are with a little "g" god.

This negotiator negotiates from one position—his! There is, in reality, no negotiation. You sell to him at his dictated demands, or he moves on to another vendor, whom, he assures you, would be happy just to be invited in on this project.

This is most often a price-driven negotiation—one in which the buying side thinks, or knows, that there is a small marketplace, and he knows, too, that many vendors out there are willing to sell. This little "g" god is using the power of competition. And he's unafraid to flaunt it.

In truth, in most negotiations, the buying side can and does use the power of competition to its advantage, and nothing is wrong with using that tactic to your advantage. That's what this book is about.

Using this or any other tactic to your advantage is not only a good negotiating strategy, but also intelligent negotiating. The difference between intelligent and advantage negotiating and the tactics of the little "g" god, use of the competition, is that this is the only tool he uses. And he or she pushes it to the extreme. We might wish to call this "Extreme Procurement"—one in which the only deal is my deal extreme emphasis on the "my."

What can you do? You could give in. That's exactly what this negotiator wants. That is where his power comes from—in the knowledge that you are agreeing with him. He gets you thinking, *there is much competition, and if I want this deal, I have to concede.* What starts as one concession from you, however, quickly escalates to your caving in on everything and walking away almost wishing that you had no deal.

Think about that. What if you had no deal? That alone might be a powerful position, and an extreme defense for you to take.

*Walk!* Walk, and don't look back. If you walk, you show the little "g" god negotiator that you are unwilling to deal or to negotiate with a non-negotiator. Walking shows your resolve. It signals that you are not giving in. Walking away from the little "g" god negotiator is the most powerful defense you have.

What if, however, you cannot walk away? What if you must make this deal work? Do this—*gain information*. Learn as much as you possibly can about this negotiator and the organization behind him. Again, in gaining information, you gain power. There, indeed, might be ways to limit this buyer's power. Remember the shut up or *Think Before You Speak* rule and *Ask*. By asking and listening, you might gain much information—and power.

Ask—does this little "g" god negotiator have all the power? Would any of the following elements affect this negotiator's ability to buy from the competition?

- Time

- Location

- Management

- Capacity

- Quality

- Needs

- Terms and Conditions

- Government Restrictions

- Laws

- History

Can this buyer use the competition against you? Can he go to the competition to buy the product or service for which he is negotiating? Ask about some of the above elements, and you indeed might find that he cannot.

If you face the task of negotiating with a little "g" god negotiator, your back is up against the wall, and you must close this deal, ask and listen. You might be unable to change the course of this negotiation drastically, but at least, you will better understand the buying side's positions and be able to use that information in later negotiations.

Don't just cave in to the little "g" god by agreeing with this negotiator. Have a plan before you get to the negotiating table on how to deal with this negotiator. Most important, when dealing with the little "g" god negotiator, know what you will do if you cannot make a deal. At least then, if you do have to give in to the little "g" god negotiator's demands, you have gained some knowledge—knowledge that is power. It might be power you cannot use in this negotiation, but power you will use in future negotiations.

## The STF Factor

What is STF? *Screw Them First*. Is there a time and place to use this tactic? Perhaps. Is there a risk in using this tactic? Perhaps. Should you ever use a tactic such as this? Definitely.

In today's "Win-Win" negotiating strategies, few organizations or negotiators would ever think of using the STF strategy. Would you? I would argue that there are times you should be prepared to use STF. Arguably, this tactic also will surely be used against you at some point. Then, it befits all negotiators to realize this tactic's possible use by you and against you.

For example, an organization you are negotiating with has just announced a horrendous third quarter loss. This announcement alone suggests that the other side might have been using STF on you already. Why? Perhaps you've been in the negotiation with them for some time or perhaps the negotiations have just started. Either way, it would be difficult to believe that the negotiators for the other side did not know of the pending announcement.

Think about it. If they knew that their company was not doing well and did not tell you of it or make you aware of the possibility of this announcement coming out while you were in negotiations, they were trying to screw you first. The other side is well aware that if you knew of the pending announcement, you would have used that announcement against them. So instead of being screwed, they were going to screw you first. Harsh? Yes. Does it happen? All the time.

The negotiating team from the troubled company would like to continue the negotiations with you, despite the recent news of their third quarter loss. During the negotiations, you learn that the other side's organization did not have just a bad third quarter, but they are preparing to file for reorganization. This is, again, another excellent opportunity for this near bankrupt company's negotiators to use the STF tactic ... on you!

Consider this. Is there the possibility here that any deal you negotiate with this near bankrupt company might fall through? Or, if this is a buying organization, might they take possession of a partial shipment of your product and then fail to pay and place your organization on their claimant list? You bet.

On the other side, is there an opportunity here for you and your organization to get all you can from the near bankrupt organization up front? Or maybe charge a dramatically higher price with fewer services and warranties? Sure there is. You have the advantage in this negotiation. After all, who will want to negotiate with this near bankrupt company?

In truth, quite a few organizations might negotiate with them, but your job is to make the other side believe that no one other than your organization will come to the table with them—not now, and perhaps not for a long time. Because you are there, you are their best and perhaps, only, source. The moral of the story—it is possible for both companies in this example to try to screw the other side first. Is this an ethical practice? I'll let you decide.

Now, to be fair, you and your negotiating team should have done your homework on this organization. If you had, you might have known the troubles the other side faced, and this announcement would not have come as a big surprise. You would have been prepared to deal with them, and perhaps, with the knowledge you had from your research and mock negotiations, you would have planned to use STF?

## Stop Saying Yes – Negotiate!

I write of this tactic, not so much so *you* plan to use it, instead, so you are prepared for its use against you. How would you know whether some sales or purchasing negotiator intends to use STF? Difficult to answer. It depends on the current position, of both sides, and perhaps, what the negotiating history is between you. That's why it should be planned.

Is there a defense to Screw Them First? Yes. If you feel someone is trying to use the STF tactic, walk! Walk away from that negotiation. Walking will give you time to analyze the situation—if you haven't done your homework. If, however, you have done your homework, and you are prepared for the use of this tactic on you, when the other side tries to screw you first, take a break from the negotiations. Tell the other side that you are going to break, but don't go back to the table.

How is this different from walking? In walking, there is no intent to return to the negotiations. In taking a break, you tell the other side that you and your negotiating team intend to return. If you take a break and do not return to the negotiations, you play on the other side's time pressures. This is a reverse STF. The net effect—you are

# Stop Saying Yes – Negotiate!

using the STF Factor against them!

## Ethical Flexibility

If I asked you if using the STF Factor, which we covered in the previous chapter, was ethical, how would you respond? Some, I'm sure, would say no, without a moment's hesitation. Others would argue that there is a time and place for it. I suggest that those who consider *all* options in *all* negotiations, without dismissing them outright, are the better negotiators. It benefits you to ponder all tactics and strategies in negotiations. Now, whether it benefits you to use them is another story.

For example, is lying during a negotiation an acceptable tactic? Is it possible that the other side is lying? Are you? What determines how far one must go during any negotiation to have the other side consider it a lie? As many people, at as many seminars, workshops, and lectures I've given over the last few years, have asked these questions a thousand times, and the answers are varied.

Is a misstatement of the facts a lie? In everyday life, you might—we might—say yes. But, during a negotiation, would the same people say that a misstatement of facts, or stretching the truth a bit, is a lie? I doubt it. During any negotiation, facts are stated or, perhaps, misstated to drive a point home. Because this is a negotiation, most would agree that we have some flexibility, some *Ethical Flexibility*.

Ethical Flexibility is a bit of a "gray area." During any negotiation, both sides use it. Consider the following:

• The buying side does not come right out and give the salesperson the true top-dollar figure they are willing to spend. Ethical Flexibility?

• The sales side does not start the negotiation by offering the lowest price they are authorized to take. Ethical Flexibility?

Would you agree then, that we enter the negotiation based on the knowledge that neither side is truthful? If so, is the other side lying? Is your side lying? Or is it all an accepted negotiating practice?

If we can agree that all negotiations are conducted with Ethical Flexibility, when then is one side or the other lying and not using Ethically Flexible? For the selling side, I would say this:

**A total misrepresentation by the selling side of the abilities of a product or service would be a lie.**

On the other hand, would it be considered a lie for the buying side to offer a total misrepresentation of the ability of the competition to meet or match the product or service being offered? The answer, based on the comments of those on both sides, would be a surprising no. The use of the competition by the procurement side to persuade the selling side to lower the price is acceptable, even if the statement is a stretch of the competition's true abilities.

If you're thinking that there is a bit of a double standard here, you're right. It can be justified, however. And that justification lies in the fact *that a misrepresentation by the selling side of the capabilities of its products or service can cause either physical or monetary harm to the buying side.* Therefore, that would constitute a lie.

However, the procurement side's stretch of the truth about the seller's competition might result in the loss of a sale, but would cause no harm, either physical or otherwise, to any person or organization. Therefore, no lie.

## Greedy/Stingy/Selfish

What's wrong with being greedy?

What's wrong with being stingy?

What's wrong with being selfish?

Whenever I ask these three questions of the attendees at the workshops and seminars I've conducted, I'm always met with a bit of hesitation. People do not want to answer these questions. Or, if an attendee is willing to answer honestly, he or she will usually restrain himself or herself—afraid of what the others might think. We don't want to be thought of as greedy, as stingy, or as selfish. Why?

The answer will shock you. It's because of Mom! That's right. Your mother and my mother. All of our mothers. They did this to us. How, you ask?

Think back to when you were a child. What did Mom say to you about sharing, about being greedy or selfish? Did Mom tell you that those were good traits? I doubt it. That's where this fear began. And it's all Mom's fault! Mom had no idea that some years later, her child would have a difficult time with negotiations because she cautioned you on being greedy, stingy, and selfish.

Look at Greedy, Stingy, and Selfish this way. In any negotiation, your organization wants you to do the best you can. The organization does not want you to give away too much. Your company would like you to get as many concessions as possible and close the deal with your side doing the best that it can. Look at how *greedy* and *stingy* and *selfish* your organization wants you to be. That's right. When you go into a negotiation for your organization or for yourself, you go in: Trying not to give up much. Trying to get all you can. Trying to walk out winning.

Look at what you've been:

- Greedy—Get all you can.

- Stingy—Don't give away your money.

- Selfish—Don't give in, and don't share.

Look at that – you're being greedy, stingy, and selfish are all good things, at least as they relate to negotiations, which is especially true when it's your money! If we're talking about greedy, stingy, and selfish as a course of action during a negotiation, then there is nothing wrong and everything right with being greedy, stingy, and/or selfish.

Is there a risk here? Sure. There's risk in all negotiations and with all tactics we use in negotiations. The key here is to be as greedy, stingy, and selfish as the other side will allow. We know the common stereotype of the used car salesperson; I'm not suggesting that you come off slimy. But if you approach your negotiations, thinking and acting as greedy, stingy, and selfish as possible, then you are less likely to give away more than you should, and you are also more likely to walk away having met your goals and aspiration levels.

## The Barker

Every person reading this book has seen this negotiator in action. They were called "barkers" once. My Uncle Johnny was a barker on the carnival circuit when I was about ten years old. I did not know then that this was a negotiating tactic, strategy, or a negotiating style. What I didn't know then, watching my Uncle Johnny, I do know now, and I get a great kick out of watching this type of negotiator at work.

There are negotiating tactics and strategies, and then there are negotiating styles. The barker is a style and a tactic. In a previous chapter, we discussed Presentation Value in your negotiations and how it can affect your negotiations. I've had many barkers in the workshops and seminars I've conducted over the past several years, and the barker has become, by far, my favorite negotiator. Having one in the room is great, and I get great pleasure out of watching this type of negotiator go to work. Not, mind you, because he's a great negotiator, but because he's fun!

It starts simply enough. The barker states the facts and then asks, "Now, wouldn't that be great if you could?" Well, you think about it, and yes, you agree that it would be great. And before you know it, he's got you, which is when the barker really goes into action. He hits you with, "If you think that's great, then just look what I can do for you."

Today, we can find him standing outside the games of chance on a carnival fairway, at state fairs hawking wares, at flea markets, and on television. If you watch late-night television, you've seen the barker at work in long format commercials commonly called "infomercials." Do they work? You bet they do.

When you encounter a barker you are so caught up, you unintentionally give information away. And the barker then uses that information as a great source of power. Power that he, in time, will use against you.

We all do it. We all fall into the barker's trap. How many of you have bought knives you do not really need, the cleaner that will whiten and brighten clothes, the one-step jewelry miracle cleaner, the grout cleaner, the steamer that kills all those deadly germs, the vacuum that never loses suction, the hair trimmer that you just cannot live without, the chicken roaster that you and your family must have, the egg boiler that makes perfect soft-boiled eggs, the car waxer you need only use once in a lifetime, and the production line software that will increase productivity and your profits? The list is endless.

I have seen many fall prey to the barker. When I ask them why they gave in, I hear, "He was just so damn convincing," or "I didn't mean to buy it, but the next thing I knew we had a deal," and "He frightened the hell out of me with words of doom and gloom if I didn't have his product!" You see, the barker isn't always just a great showman who overwhelms your senses with his dramatic skills—he can be downright frightening.

I had a president of a large engineering firm in one workshop in the Detroit area who turned out to be a great negotiator. He did it, though, by using his *intimidation factor*. He was a barker to be sure, but his tactic was different. He became loud and animated. He used foul language. He pounded the desk. He stormed. He stamped. He was great fun to watch, but a bear with whom to negotiate. Most of those he did negotiate with folded and gave in. He and his antics intimidated them.

Now, a few—very few—got up and walked away.

Most did not.

Why? Because their pressures to settle were far greater than the risk of walking. In short, what this negotiator did was to find out, almost immediately, that the people he was negotiating with could not walk away from the deal. If they could have walked, they surely would have. Once he had that information, he turned it all on.

Sometimes, it's in what we *don't* do, rather than what we *do*. If you were negotiating with this negotiator and you didn't walk, he knew that there were pressures on you to close this deal. And if you did walk, this negotiator would change his tune and his tactics. He would settle down and show you a kinder and gentler side. Even then, he'd learned information about your side, and he'd shown you that if you did not cooperate in this negotiation, there was a different side of him, one you might not want to see again. Either way, he had power.

Be cautious with the barker. He might be fun to watch, but if you are caught up in his antics, you're his. So is the deal!

## The Stinky Finger

Have you ever touched something that left an unpleasant odor on your fingers? Most of us try to wash it off as soon as possible, but until we can, we all do the same thing—smell the finger to see if it still smells. A good friend developed this theory. He didn't know that this was a negotiating tactic, until I pointed it out to him. Now, he uses it all the time.

Think about a negotiation you stepped into and almost immediately thought that something was afoot. Instead of backing out of the negotiation, what do we do? That's right. Keep sniffing to see what stinks.

Some curiosity in us keeps us in the negotiation. We want to clean it up. We want to discover what the other side is up to. The trouble is that once we start to invest so much effort into figuring out what stinks, we've now negotiated ourselves into the awkward position of nearly committing to the deal. And it could be a deal that we do not want. Can't happen to you? Want to bet?

## Stop Saying Yes – Negotiate!

Have you ever been to a state fair, a carnival, or an amusement park where the barkers we discussed in a previous chapter are hawking their wares? You know the stuff—the knives, the miracle cleaners, the revolutionary diets, and those great buns and abs! What do a vast number of us do? We stop. We listen. We buy.

Now, did we necessarily believe in the product or service when we stopped? No. We stopped because we could not believe what we were hearing from the barkers. Something stinks. Do we leave? No. We listen because we want to find what stinks about this product or service. We do that so we can prove to ourselves and the others around us that we know more about the service or product than the barker does.

Instead of discovering what about this product or service we want to disprove, we begin to self-negotiate. Maybe this isn't such a bad product. Maybe I could use it, or I know someone else who might want it. If it works, I could … The self-negotiation goes on until we have negotiated ourselves into wanting or needing the product or service.

I've done it. I know my friends have done it. So have you! We can't help it. We forget that something about this product or service stinks, and instead, we negotiated with ourselves for and now we have to have it.

The barker pulls you in, and you become part of his show. Your participation in the barker's routine drives more sales or helps him make better deals for all in his favor. If you debate with him one on one or in a group setting—such as a carnival or fair—you stir up the crowd. You might try to disprove his product or service, but believe me, he has heard it all before, and if he hasn't, he is too quick to back into a corner. You debate with him, and he gets sales. You bring up questions that the crowd—or others on your negotiating team—might want to ask and he answers them and then makes you look foolish or uneducated about the product or service he's selling.

You are doing the work for him. Barkers love people like you. You bring him the crowd he needs. Or you turn your team into *his* team. The barker and the Stinky Finger are powerful tactics and styles when combined.

Don't sink time and energy, like a downed ship, into a deal you cannot afford to have. A deal that is not the right deal for you. That sunk cost of time and energy might legitimize it for you. Or the other side might use it against you.

If you sense that a deal might stink, wash it off right away. Get out of the situation. Don't try to show that you are smarter, better, or anything else. That's where you'll invest too much, and the sunk cost of that investment will consume the negotiation.

## The Risk Factor

In every negotiation that takes place, two components need to be considered about risk: the *Personal* side and the *Organizational* side. First, let's look at the negotiator—the person or persons you and perhaps your team members are negotiating with. Here, we will determine the *Personal* side of risk. To do so, we must ask this question: *Will the risk this person is willing to take, in his or her life, directly affect the amount of risk he or she is prepared to take in their negotiation with me?*

If I were a risk taker in my life, would you expect that risk-taking ability to affect my negotiating style? You and I are about to enter into a negotiation—a one-on-one negotiation. We agree to meet at my office. You walk into the office and cannot help noticing that the walls are covered with pictures of me. There's one of me skydiving, several of me bungee jumping, a scuba diving picture of my hand in a shark's mouth, and me rock climbing ... without a rope! Am I a risk taker? If so, will my risk-taking ability or tolerance affect our negotiation? The answer is ... yes. I am a risk taker in my life. It stands then that I will also be *more likely* to take *greater risk* in my professional life.

The question must also be asked of each person on the negotiator's team. Will each person's ability to assume personal risk affect your ability to negotiate with him or her? The answer is always-yes! The personal risk tolerance of someone you are negotiating with will always affect the negotiation.

If the statement, "The personal risk tolerance of someone you are negotiating with will always affect the negotiation," is true of the other side, then it must also be true for you and your side. Think about it. Have you ever considered your risk tolerance when negotiating? To get the best deal possible, you must know your own personal risk tolerance and understand the other side's personal risk tolerance.

We know people who regularly make the journey to Las Vegas or Atlantic City and wager much money on the chance they will come out ahead. We also know people who will take the same trip to Las Vegas or Atlantic City and not wager one dime, not even a nickel. Although one person is willing to bet the house—to risk it all or a goodly amount on the chance they might come out ahead—the other will tolerate little or no risk. He or she is unprepared to part with any of their hard-earned cash on a game of chance, even if the rewards can be life changing! Personal risk tolerance levels on two different ends of the spectrum.

A start-up media storage and retrieval company has just moved from some backwoods location to a Main Street building, and it is now ready to compete, big time. Is it more likely to venture into greater risk than, let's say, Microsoft or EMC? Probably. The risks here are different. For the start-up, there is less to lose and everything to gain. For Microsoft or EMC, there is much more to lose. Think of Microsoft in its infancy years in someone's garage. Was Microsoft then a risk-taking organization? Is it now a big risk taker? The more an organization has to lose, the less risk they are prepared to take. Could we argue then that this conservatism about risk tolerance will trickle down to the buying or selling divisions of this organization? I'm certain that we could say yes.

The organizational side of risk will also always affect your ability to negotiate. If the organization is conservative in its risk tolerance, so too, will be the negotiators and the general atmosphere of the negotiation. A company prepared to take great risk and, perhaps reap the rewards of risk, will have a negotiator also prepared to take risk. Here, however, is where we must factor in the personal side of risk to the organizational side.

Let us presume that you are negotiating with a risk tolerant organization, but the negotiator is not a risk taker in his personal life. Even though the organization he negotiates for might be willing to accept risk, he might not be. Thus, your negotiation with him will be different from someone who, like the organization, is willing to accept risk. Knowing the risk tolerance of the other side's organization and of your organization and understanding both your personal and the other side's personal risk tolerance can be key to your negotiation.

Risk scares us in negotiations. It is a great unknown. Yet, only three possibilities can happen about risk?

You take a shot. You risk it and lose.

You take a shot. You risk it and win.

But what is the worst that could happen?

You take no risk!

## The Family Factor

This, to me, is a fascinating question of negotiations. How does your upbringing, or the way you were raised, affect the way you negotiate? Think about it. Was your family entrepreneurial, or were you raised in a blue-collar family where punching the clock was a way of life? Are you a free-spirited, free-thinking person? Would you consider yourself very conservative? Do you accept change, or are you slow to change? What were your parents like ... as parents?

During the hundreds of seminars I've given on negotiating, I've asked this question to thousands of people, and the look on their faces as they contemplate their answers is always the same. It's the, *I've never thought of that*, look. Well, if you've never thought of this, there's no better time than now.

Ask people why they do the things they do and sooner or later—usually much sooner—you'll hear something to the effect of "My family did it that way." Logically, then, you bring this *Family Factor* into all your negotiations. And by the way, this is not scientific research, but the understanding of what goes on in the real-world negotiations that happen every day.

The effect of the Family Factor was made clear during one workshop, when I had split the group of attendees into small teams for a mock negotiation. The teams were then sent off on their own to plan their negotiation. Not long into the planning phase of the mock negotiation, an older man came up to me and asked me if I would put him with another team. I asked him why, and he responded with, "The kids that I'm with don't know a thing about the real world."

The "Generation X" types that made up this man's team were not very concerned with what would happen if the negotiation did not work out. Sure, they wanted to conclude the deal with an outcome they could live with, but if they didn't, they said that it would be easy enough to take a different course of action. They were not over concerned. In their planning, the Gen X-ers were prepared to give away some key concessions to build a better relationship with the other side. The older man, as it turned out, was raised during the height of the Depression and almost all his decisions were based on what happened during the Depression, and how they had to live with the few necessities available. His negotiations were primarily based on the question of "What if there is no deal?" To him, a relationship with the other side was important, but not as important as having made the best deal possible without giving in on concessions. It was more of a "pinch and save" negotiation, born in the Great Depression.

The Gen X-ers were more concerned with building a relationship that would see them through future negotiations. The thinking was that the future was bright for the Gen X-ers, while the future was uncertain for the older man. Both types of negotiations were based on different attitudes of life, which takes the Family Factor one step further. Not only is your family affecting the way you negotiate, but your peers and your generation also affect your negotiations.

Take this into account when you plan your next negotiation— not only the effect your Family Factor has on you, but also the effect the Family Factor will have on the other side. Plan your negotiation to counter your own Family Factor instincts and, perhaps, limitations. Consider the influence of the Family Factor on the other side.

## The Emotional Negotiator

Most of us have witnessed this type of negotiator. If you don't think that you have, read on, and you'll recognize him instantly. This person tries to appeal to your sense of "good." His ploy is to convince you that if you do "good" by him, he'll look good to his management, and he promises the next time he'll make it up to you, and you'll look like the hero.

He's the negotiator who will latch on to your desire to help a fellow human. You see, if you don't close this deal with him now, at the price he needs to close, he'll lose his bonus. That will mean that his kid will be unable to finish this semester at college, and that would be too bad because his kid had a bad childhood. In addition, his wife—whom, he tells you, he's already having marital problems with, but is trying to work it out—will surely leave him. What would his kid do then?

Usually, now, he'll take out some pictures of the wife and kids, and perhaps the dog or the cat they rescued from the shelter. You'll be sure to notice a tear in his eye as he tells you about the struggle that poor little cat had to go through before he was saved by his family. He'll tell you about the veterinarian who wanted to put the cat to sleep, but he would have none of it. It cost him, but no dollar amount could have prevented him from saving that poor little creature. Now, it's important to note, that if you don't like cats, he'll make it about a puppy, a turtle, a bird, an iguana, or whatever you let him know you care.

You see what's happening here? It's about whatever emotion he can bring out in you. Once he's found your emotional weak spot, he's going to pounce on it.

We've all been there, or we know someone close to us who has been there. And because we most likely have, and we wouldn't ever want to see someone else go through what _____ (you fill in the blank of the friend, relative, or acquaintance) went through, our sense of emotional justice takes over, and we give in.

That's what this negotiator wants. It's so easy for us to fall into this person's trap, because most of us are good, caring humans. We *self-negotiate* into believing we are helping this person, and in some sense, making the world a better place.

How do you counter this negotiator? Best bet might be to walk away. Don't become involved. Let him know clearly that this negotiation tactic will not work on you. When this negotiator starts to move into the emotional state of negotiation, end it. Tell him that you feel bad for his position, but his personal position does not, and will not, affect the way you make your decisions.

Wish him luck, but move on with the negotiation. Direct the conversation away from the emotional side and back to the facts. Once this negotiator has learned that you're on to his tactics, he'll move on—not that he won't try to come back to it. You must stay vigilant with the Emotional Negotiator. After all, he works on emotions. We all have them, and we all let them show at some point. He knows it, and he's just waiting.

To better help you understand where you stand on Emotional Negotiating, ask yourself how you would handle the following situation. Be honest.

You're deep into a heated negotiation. Things are not going well for the other side. You're feeling great that you are getting all the concessions you asked for, and you've had to give up almost nothing. You know that you are going to be the hero when you get back to the office. Just as you and the other side are about to sign the contract to close this deal, the negotiator you're working with breaks down in tears, sobbing, uncontrollable tears. This negotiator tells you of all the problems that will come because of the bad deal that's being signed. More tears follow.

Now, if the negotiator you're working with is a woman, and you are a man, how do you feel? How do you respond? What if you are a man and the negotiator you're negotiating with is a man? Do you respond differently? And a woman negotiating with a woman? Do we get another response?

This might not be politically correct thinking, but you must know how you will respond to different situations in negotiations— even if it's politically incorrect to ask. If you haven't prepared for this, you might find yourself about to close an unbelievable deal, only to be hit with a last minute barrage of sobs and tears, and it might all be an act by the Emotional Negotiator (Presentation Value) to turn around the deal.

## The Intellectual Negotiator

This negotiator is much like the Emotional Negotiator we discussed in the previous chapter. He wants to do right by you, so he can do right for the world. He's an intellect. He knows what he's talking about, and you wouldn't dare question him. He has your best interest in mind. He wouldn't be where he is now if he didn't know what he was doing. You've heard this negotiator before. He'll say, "Believe me, I've been doing this since you were in diapers …" or "I remember when I was wet behind the ears like you …" or "Why don't you just listen? Maybe you'll learn something." He tells you that he wants everyone to be happy. No matter what it takes, he's going to make sure that you're happy, your boss is happy, the boss's boss is happy, the neighbors are happy, your mother is happy … The list goes on. Now, don't forget he wants all the same for himself, his boss, his mother, and his neighbor.

How is he going to do this? How is he going to make a deal with you that everyone will be happy to get? He promises that you will leave with a deal your boss will love—your neighbor and your mother too—if only they could get a deal like this. He'll continue with a statement similar to "Not everyone can get this deal, you see, but you can, and only you can. And to do this, you must act now."

Starting to sound familiar? The Intellectual Negotiator approaches you with a "we can make the world a better place if you accept this deal" attitude. The problem is that he's asking you to accept *his* deal.

This deal he's asking you to accept to make everyone happy is not a deal you have negotiated from a position of power, but one that has been negotiated from a position of guilt, inadequacy, embarrassment, or doubt. You might begin to think the Intellectual Negotiator is so much more intelligent than you are, and because this negotiator is so intelligent, he would never offer a deal less than you need. His rules. His description.

The Intellectual Negotiator plays—or should I say—preys on those who let on (give away) that they do not have all the facts and are somewhat unsure on the specifics of the product or service negotiated. This negotiator is much like the professor at college with whom no one dared disagree. Why didn't anyone disagree? Because the professor wrote the book on whatever subject (a product or service) you're talking about, and no one questions him. Then, why would you? That's the question the negotiator will ask, and if you're not sure of your position in this negotiation, you might just give him the answer he wants to hear.

The Intellectual Negotiator is only as intelligent as you are stupid. Sorry, but it's the truth. You let on to him that there is a hole in your armor, and he's all over it.

Don't become combative. Instead, remember the *Think Before You Speak* rule. Listen and respond with appropriate answers. Don't let him lead you astray. If all else fails, and you think you are falling into this negotiator's trap, stop the negotiation. Agree with him that he is too much for you and tell him that you need a break, so you can call in your boss, coworker, or another expert on your product to conclude the negotiation with him. I guarantee that he will change his tune with you. And you might just find that, perhaps, he isn't so intelligent after all!

## Say No!—Then Say It Again

You have a buyer, or you have a seller. He's committed. You can close the deal right this second, and you and your organization would be in great shape. The other side wants to close. What do you do? You say no! That's right. You say no.

Why would anyone want to say no when this deal—and it's a deal you or I could live with and even be excited about—is about to be closed? There is a simple answer to the question of why? By saying no and not closing now, you could get a better deal.

Just because you *can* close the deal now does not mean that you *should*. There is usually a better deal to be had. The problem is that most of us settle because we are in sight of our own targets or aspirations. Or, more especially, we are in sight of our own *limiting* targets or aspirations. There might be a better deal to be had if we had just said no. We must say no, not only to those we are negotiating with, but also to ourselves. Say no to your self-negotiations.

We don't want to say no for so many reasons. The one I hear

the most is, "Why should I put myself and/or my team at risk by not closing the deal now when the other side is perfectly willing and able to close?" Because there is more to be had.

Most of us are happy to settle. It's easy. No more work, and the deal is done. In truth, the deal isn't finished; we have simply concluded it. More was to be had from this deal if we had just held out a little longer and said no at least once again.

And don't stop there; say no once more. Say it again. And again.

Frightening tactic to use? Sure. It can be. It can also add much to the satisfaction level of the other side and enhance the negotiation overall.

You have the other side in the Yes Zone, and as we will discuss in the next chapter, once you have the other side in the *Yes Zone,* you can usually get more. There's risk, sure. You might alienate the other side by pushing. But if you don't push a little, you'll never know how far you could have gone.

Saying no might have an ironic effect on the other side—they might leave the negotiation happier that they paid more or that they sold for less. Why? Because you worked them on the deal. They got the best out of the negotiation they felt they could because you were able to and ready to say no.

Now, the other side can go to their bosses and colleagues feeling confident that they got a good deal. That is, they can now sell themselves (self-negotiate) on the presumption that you were prepared to say no again.

## The Yes Zone

If you're not sure about saying no and then saying it again when you have a deal that by all accounts is a great deal, then you might prefer the thinking in the *Yes Zone*. That is, once you have the other side in the *Yes Zone*, hit them again.

When is a negotiator most vulnerable? Just after he or she has said yes. Once you have a yes from the other side, they have already adjusted their targets and aspiration levels. They are now doing your work for you. They have been, and are, self-negotiating. And, my friends, that is a good thing.

I saw this at work recently at a jewelry store where a man was carefully eyeing the luxury watches. He had his eye on a very nice Movado. The retail price on the watch was just about eleven hundred dollars. A clerk approached, commenting on how nice Movado watches were. Next, without asking if the customer cared to look at a watch more closely, the clerk removed one from the case and handed it to the man. I listened closely as the clerk began to ask the customer a series of questions, all peppered into a conversation about high-end watches and how impressive Movado watches are especially for the price.

Soon, the clerk learned that the customer had just received a raise and wanted to treat himself to something special. After a moment's thought, the customer chose a watch. The clerk congratulated the customer on a great selection. He even invited the other clerks in the store to congratulate the customer, which the entire staff did, wholeheartedly. The customer beamed.

Without skipping a beat, the clerk said how nice it was to buy something that was not only a congratulation gift for a job well done, but also a gift that was so useful. "Who could argue with that?" the clerk asked.

"My wife," the customer responded.

Again, our clerk was right there. "Well, sir," he said, "she wouldn't complain if you brought one home for her also."

The customer left with two new Movado watches: one for him and one for his wife.

What else is your customer ready to buy or negotiate away to you? You might never know, unless you get them when they are in the

*Yes Zone.*

## Limit Your Authority

Just because you can close a deal does not mean that you should close the deal. We discussed earlier, saying no and then saying it again. Limiting Your Authority is an example of saying no, without using the word *no*.

Many on the sales side would argue that when you're at the close, "Close 'em." In general, that would be true. However, it is worth noting that not every opportunity to close now is the right opportunity to close now. And your ability to close—that is, the authority you have to close the deal—might not be in your best interest. Or, more especially, it might not be in your best interest to give the other side the information that you *can* close this deal.

Too often those on the sales side say that they must have the ability to close or the buying side will not want to work with them. In some cases, that might be true. The question is who determines the way you're selling organization sells? You? Or the buying side?

If the terms and conditions of any negotiation between you

and another organization are to follow these procedures: salesperson, then sales manager, and final approval by the regional manager, then that is the procedure the buying side must follow. Your rules. Not theirs.

All too often, the selling side is ready to give in to the demands of those on the buying side, without first qualifying those demands. For instance, would the buying side not buy from your organization because it must deal with the salesperson first, then the sales manager, and then a final OK by the regional manager? You might say yes. Then I would ask, "Have you ever tested this?" And when I do ask this question, this is what I hear. "Not really."

The problem with authority in negotiations is that we use that authority. We must ask ourselves if it would be better not to use it or at least to allow the other side to believe that we do not have that authority. Limiting our authority forces the other side to spend time—time they might not have. That's power to you.

You're negotiating with a buying organization, and they say that they must close this deal today. You tell them, no problem; you have the authority to close the deal. Great, for the other side, that is.

They have now played on your time limits. That's right, *your* time limits. How?

They have given you a time restriction you did not have when you came into this negotiation. They took power away from you. Or, more accurately, you gave your power away. If they don't like the deal, they can say no and play on the negotiation's time constraints—the time constraints they have imposed on this negotiation because they know that you have the authority to close this deal. You must close with them today, they have just told you, or they will move on. Your problem ... you told them that *you could* close.

Now, what would have happened if the other side had told you that they must close this deal with you today, or they would have to move to the next seller? Only this time, you responded by saying, "You must have your vice president sign off on the final deal?"

Can the other side walk? Sure. Did you learn something for future negotiations if they do walk? Sure, again.

On the other hand, what if they don't walk? New questions should arise.

- Do they have to close now, or was this a time tactic?

- What if they said that they could not wait for your VP to sign off, and you hit them with the fact that you have your VP on the way? How would they react?

- Are you stalling?

- Were they stalling?

We love authority, and we love to use it, which could be your downfall in a negotiation. Having authority is a great power, but a greater power is to have authority and not use it. Be prepared in your next negotiation to *Limit Your Authority*.

## Legitimize Your Position

Question: What one little word can cause so much trouble in negotiations? Answer: Why?

In our negotiations, other than *no*, *why* is the most powerful word. It's easy to ask, and it gets the other side talking. And we know that when the other side talks and we listen, we gain power.

Most of us are not prepared properly to use the why question. And why would that be? Because most why questions are answered before we ever get a chance to ask them.

Example:  You're on the beach, no shirt, and no shoes. You decide to walk into a restaurant to grab a bite to eat. Will they serve you? We've all seen the sign—No Shirt, No Shoes, No Service. So, we put on our shirts and shoes before we walk in. But if we were in a negotiation, and the other side said to you, "No Shirt, No Shoes, No Negotiation …" you would immediately ask why?

How does your dress affect the negotiation? Now, I realize that there is little opportunity to enter into a business negotiation without wearing a shirt or shoes, but if one did present itself, and the other side said, "No Shirt, No Shoes, No Negotiation . . . " wouldn't you ask, why? In the restaurant, however, we don't ask because we think we know the answer. The restaurant management legitimizes their position with health codes. How do you fight that?

In your negotiations, you, too, must *Legitimize Your Position*.

- "It's what everyone pays."

- "That's our standard rate."

- "We never give discounts."

- "It's on the price list."

We've all heard these words or some statements similar to them. They are powerful tools to the negotiator. What they do is legitimize the pricing structure and your position.

In your strategies, spend time discovering what legitimizes your price and position. Find answers to the why question, and then say them before the other side can ask the why questions. This approach will stop any further why questions from being asked. Now, like the sign that read No Shirt, No Shoes, No Service, you have *Legitimized Your Position*.

## Funny Money—Give It Value

Credit cards, checking accounts, casino match play offers, coupons, rebates, special sales, limited time offers, discounts, commissions, and bonuses—what do they share? They are money to us.

Now, what are they worth? What is the value of that discount, coupon, or limited time sale? That depends on how much value it holds for the other side. Notice, I did not say, how much is it worth to you? I said, "How much value does it hold for the other side?" None? A little? A great deal? Now, here's where you come in to the equation. It only has value to the other side if you give it value.

A limited time offer might have no value to you if you don't want what they're offering. Limited time sale or not, if you don't want the product or service, the sale could go on for eternity, and you're still not going to buy.

I'm selling a grand piano, and I tell you that you can have it for $3,000, but you must buy now. Three grand is a great price, but if you live in a five-story, walk-up studio apartment in New York City, the limited time to buy at $3,000 doesn't mean much. Thus, there is no value in this limited time offer. However, if you're a piano tuner, and you come upon this deal, you might jump at it because you know many people who might wish to buy this piano from you. For one person, there is no value in the time-restricted offer. For the other, there is great value. *You must qualify your target before you make any Funny Money offer.*

I hate those rebate coupons that so many manufacturers offer. I'm of the opinion that if a manufacturer is going to offer a discount or sale price, they should just offer it. Why don't they? Because we (you, me, and everyone else who buys with these rebates or coupons) have given them value. The problem is that we (and the seller of the product knows this) seldom take advantage of the rebates. The result is a sale with a discount that never happens because we fail to act. It is a brilliant marketing strategy, but I hate it nonetheless.

What happens when we offer a *Funny Money* concession when we have not qualified the other side? For one, we have given information away, and that information is … that's right, power!

When a *Funny Money* concession is offered to an unqualified buyer or seller, we are telling them that there is room to negotiate. A negotiation that they might not have expected, or even considered, until we were kind enough to hand it to them.

As a buyer, *Funny Money* can cause you to spend more than you normally would. And as a seller, *Funny Money* can cause you to give away more than you normally would. Either way, if it does not have value, then it costs you too much.

## Free Costs Too Much

How much is free? Most would reply, "Free has no cost." Free implies that it has no cost. Yet, to you, free can be expensive. A current advertising trend makes this point perfectly, and I'll bet that many of you have seen these commercials, and perhaps, some of you have even taken the bait and bought one of these "free" items. How do you buy something that's free, you might ask. Like this.

I offer you a product— a pill to control your carbohydrate cravings and, thus, help you lose weight. You are likely to be interested in this product. After all, who is not trying to control his or her weight? Or, who doesn't know someone who is? If you cannot use this great discovery, then I'm sure you know someone who would benefit from it.

Now, I tell you that the 30-day supply costs only $59.00. For that price, you might take a chance on buying this product for yourself, but for $59.00, you're probably not going to take a chance and buy it for someone else, especially when you're not even sure that these pills will control your carbohydrate cravings. Then, I add, you not only get one bottle of this breakthrough product, a 30-day supply, but I'll give you *two* bottles, a 60-day supply, or enough for you and a friend to share, all for the same price of $59.00 ... sounding better?

But wait! Now, I will give you both bottles, a 60-day supply of carbohydrate control pills, free. That's right. Free.

Who wouldn't take them? Most of us would. Why not? They're free. And in this case, free has how much value? Right. None.

Free has no value whatsoever. Why is that? Because the seller of this product did not give it any value. True, it does have an established selling price of $59.00, and it could be argued that the price structure gives it value. It establishes a benchmark. But for whom? The seller. The price structure gives it value to the one selling the product, but the price of $59.00 does not give the product any value to the buyer. Why? Because it's free. You'll take as many as I'm giving, even if you never plan to use it ... because it's free!

But wait again! What if I, the seller of these miracle carbohydrate-controlling pills, added one more element to the deal? What if I told you that you could have, not one, not two, but three bottles of these miracle pills free, that all you do is pay for the shipping and handling that is just $4.95 each?

Are the carbohydrate control pills still free? Some might say, yes. The answer is no. They are not free. They are now costing you $4.95 each. But guess what? They now have value to you. You are getting a $60.00 product, which you could use, for only $5.00. Are the pills worth the five bucks to you?

Now, we have just learned something from those who do not want the pills for five bucks. We've learned that they never wanted them. They were only going to take them because the product was free and had no value. And for those who would spend the five dollars, we have determined:

- They want the product, and they are not just accepting something with no cost to it.

- They are willing to invest in themselves or others.

- They need to lose weight, or they know someone who does.

- They are potential leads for future sales.

- They are great prospects for collateral products.

Think about how much "free" has cost you. As a buyer. As a seller.

In your lives, do you spend more when you use a credit card or when you pay with cash? It's been proved repeatedly that credit is a catalyst for us to spend. Does it have value? Sure. It enables us to get that new computer or big screen TV now and not have to pay for it for 60, 90, 180 days, or longer. We have it now, can enjoy it now, and don't have to pay for it for days to come.

What a great idea. The seller can reduce inventory, record a sale, and the buyer gets the product he wants now.

Does it have a cost? Sure. Credit costs; that's why it's offered. Most buyers will not pay in full, as the contract states. Thus, finance charges set in. For the seller, there's value in establishing a relationship with a customer and, perhaps, creating customer loyalty.

Free and *Funny Money* go hand in hand in negotiations. They can be paired to form a convincing concession. But beware of the true costs of free and unqualified *Funny Money* concessions.

## Every Asset Has a Liability

Don't overlook your self-imposed pressures. I'm the seller of a product, and I have a sole source position. I don't have to sell to you; you have little, if any, choice on where to buy.

You want my product. You need my product. You have to buy my product. A wonderful asset for the seller, wouldn't you say?

Let's look at this. You're in the market for a new car. You've checked out the new-car dealerships, but a friend suggests that you try a used car with low mileage. I have an advertisement in the local paper that catches your eye, "An almost new, two-year-old vehicle with virtually no miles on it." You check it out, and sure enough, the vehicle is in pristine condition with just a few hundred miles on it. Other vehicles of this make, model, and year are selling for a few thousand less than the one I'm selling. But the mileage on those cars is way up, and they're not in the same pristine condition as the one I have for sale.

In this case, I am a sole source of this like new, low-mileage vehicle. Your job as the buyer of this vehicle is to turn the selling side's *assets* into *liabilities*. Where is the liability in the nearly new car with low mileage, in like new condition, being sold at a good price?

Ask yourself some questions.

- Why is the mileage so low?

- Why hasn't the car been driven?

- Why is the price so competitive?

- What's wrong with the vehicle?

- What's up with the owner?

In business negotiations, what could be a liability with a *Sole-Source* seller?

- Well, for one, the sole-source position can be or could be interpreted as a liability.

- What if the company runs into financial trouble?

- Or the raw materials used to manufacture the product become scarce or very expensive?

- What if the selling side cannot deliver?

A question you need to ask both your organization and the

other side is do you and your organization want to deal with a sole

source company that could place your organization in jeopardy? Their

Their asset just became a  liability.

Every asset either the selling side or the buying side presents to

you has a liability to it. Don't allow your self-imposed pressures to get

in the way of finding that liability and using it to your advantage.

## Negotiating for Outcome, Not for Satisfaction

Far too often, we negotiate not for satisfaction, but for the outcome. We want to close the deal. If the negotiation is only about the outcome, we possibly close the deal with both, our side and the other side, very unsatisfied. What we fail to do when rushing to close the deal is to consider the *Satisfaction Levels*.

Is it possible to close the deal with the other side where they pay more than they originally planned to pay and come out of the deal feeling more satisfied than if they had paid less? Could you close a deal where you received the highest numbers you had hoped to receive, yet leave feeling as though there was something more? Something left out of the deal? Something that you could have done better?

Concentrating on the outcome of the deal, that is the close, and not the satisfaction level of the deal, can be futile. We close. We both win. We are both unsatisfied.

How do we win yet remain unsatisfied? For one, we entered the negotiation with our chief goal to close at a predetermined price and set of concessions. If we achieve that goal, then we have won. And if the other side has also reached its goals and aspiration levels, then they, too, have won. A Win-Win negotiation. Yet, both sides might well walk away from that negotiation feeling as though there was something more to be had.

- More time

- A greater discount

- An exclusive

- An add-on or bundled product

- No freight or shipping charges

- The right of first refusal on coming products

These are just a few simple examples of what can cause us to be unsatisfied with an end deal that we closed in our aspiration levels.

Let's put it this way on a personal level. A company with which you have wanted to work has just hired you. It has been your goal to gain a position with this company for some time and your plan is to grow and climb the ladder of this company. You have been hired with a $10,000 increase in your salary over your previous position. You're ecstatic! Ten thousand more will mean much to your family.

## Stop Saying Yes – Negotiate!

On the first day of work, you meet another new employee in orientation. During a casual conversation, you learn that this other new employee—who will be performing the same job duties you will—makes $2,000 more than you. Are you satisfied with your job?

In this personal negotiation, you had achieved everything you set out to do. You reached you aspiration levels, but the result is an unsatisfied conclusion. You could have gotten more.

Why didn't you get more? Could be that you did not work hard enough in the negotiation. In every negotiation, work the other side. I've said it before. Just because you *can* say yes does not mean that you *should* say yes.

How would the negotiation for this new position have ended if you had hesitated in saying yes? What would have changed if you made the other side—in this case, the prospective employer—work a little harder?

As you're about to close any negotiation, stop and ask yourself if closing now will bring you and, even more important, the other side satisfaction.

## Perceived Win-Win?

So much has been said about Win-Win Negotiations in many other publications, and it seems the catchphrase for all negotiations today, so I need not write much about Win-Win here.

Instead, let me clear up what is the biggest misconception about Win-Win negotiations.

Let me start by asking what you want from any negotiation. Is your goal to take it all? Let the other side take it all? Or, do you want a negotiation that, when completed, leaves both sides getting exactly what they intended to?

If you, like most people, said that the latter is what you want from a negotiation—both sides getting exactly what they intended to—then, would you call that a Win-Win Negotiation?

Why? Or, perhaps, why not?

If both sides have left the negotiating table with everything they intended to get, then it must be said that was a Win and a Win. Is there anything wrong with that? If you're the negotiator for my organization, and you said, "No, nothing is wrong with that," I don't want you on my team. Why?

If I define Win-Win as both sides walking out of a negotiation having met their self-imposed aspiration levels or targets, then Win-Win is easy. I lower my aspiration levels to the lowest level I can, and you do the same. When the negotiation is over, we have both met and, possibly, exceeded our aspiration levels. Thus, a Win-Win. The problem is we both lost.

I do not want members of my team to negotiate for Win-Win. Why? Because that negotiator is prepared to lower his or her aspiration levels to meet the other side's lowered targets and aspirations.

A *True Win-Win Negotiation* philosophy should be summed up this way: *I want the other side to leave the negotiation believing they got all concessions available and giving up only those concessions they believe they had to give up to close the deal.* The important word in the preceding definition is *believe.* I want the other side to believe they have closed this negotiation with Win-Win. But I don't want Win-Win.

Is that fair? Win-Win has nothing to do with being fair. I'm afraid that this is where too many negotiators get into trouble—trying to be fair. Most negotiators, after thinking about it for a bit, realize that they do not want a Win-Win Negotiation. They want a, *my side won, but the other side thinks that they've won,* negotiation.

Then, what we want at the close of a negotiation is a *Perceived Win-Win,* which is where the other side has the perception that they did not give away much and believes they have walked out the winner. They are satisfied. We are satisfied.

Equally so? No. The other side thinks we closed with a Win-Win Negotiation. We know differently.

Now, **Stop Saying Yes ... Negotiate!**

## About the Author

Richard Devin has conducted negotiating workshops and seminars in the United States, Canada and Mexico. A sought after speaker and negotiating motivator, he has worked with Fortune 500 companies for the past 10 years, inspiring both inside and outside sales departments, purchasing and communications to better negotiations.

Devin negotiated for top Los Angeles talent as a Theatrical Talent Agent at two of LA's top agencies. His clients included Academy Award, Grammy Award and Emmy Award winning and nominated actors and performers. He now lives and works in Las Vegas, Nevada as a gaming executive.

Devin is a contributing writer for Envy Man magazine, Southern Nevada Equestrian magazine and is the published author of two business books to the showbiz trade: Actors' Resumes: The Definitive Guidebook (Players Press, 2002) and Do You Want To Be An Actor? 101 Answers to Your Questions About Breaking Into the Biz (13Thirty Books, 2013). His novel, Ripper – A Love Story (13Thirty Books, 2013) has reached critical acclaim. He is a produced and award winning playwright: My Mother's Coming (Money Shot Productions, Hollywood CA).

www.ingramcontent.com/pod-product-compliance
Lightning Source LLC
Chambersburg PA
CBHW060040210326
41520CB00009B/1200